Peace Through Covert Means

History is a blood-stained saga. From ancient empires to the modern nation-states, the annals of time are filled with conquest and cruelty. Wars have raged across continents, empires have risen and fallen, and entire civilizations have vanished into obscurity. Leaders and generals have wielded armies as instruments of power, sweeping across borders and spilling oceans of blood. For every fleeting moment of peace, there are a hundred stories of devastation, of victory claimed through violence, and lives lost in battles that left the land scarred and its people haunted.

At times, diplomacy has achieved a fragile truce, a temporary reprieve from the devastation. Yet these moments of calm are rare. History's pages are littered with broken treaties and shattered promises, as nations return to old grudges and fight for supremacy. Peace secured through negotiation demands patience and trust—qualities that are often scarce on the world stage. For every success story in diplomacy, countless others have fallen apart, swept away by greed, ambition, or simple mistrust. The reality of history is bleak: peace, when it arrives, is often a fragile and fleeting illusion.

But there is a third option, one that doesn't rely on the high ideals of diplomacy or demand the sacrifices of brutal warfare. This option exists in the shadows, quietly working beyond the public eye, and it has its own secret heroes: the spies and covert operatives who navigate a world hidden from the headlines. These men and women are not often celebrated, their names unknown to history, yet their impact on the world is undeniable. Through their skill and sacrifice, wars have been averted, lives have been saved, and the delicate balance of peace has been preserved.

Covert action is that hidden force—an alternative path that allows nations to defend their interests without the brutal calculus of open warfare. It is the art of influence and deception, practiced by operatives who act not for glory or recognition but for a higher calling. These covert operatives are the shadow soldiers, the unacknowledged defenders of peace. They move silently, altering the course of events with precision, manipulating outcomes, and pulling strings behind the scenes to avert disaster. In a world defined by war and conquest, they are the guardians of an unseen peace.

For those who understand the stakes, covert action is not merely an alternative; it is a vital necessity. There are moments in history when a nation's survival hangs by a thread, when a single misstep could plunge the world into chaos. In these moments, covert operatives become the last line of defense, stepping into the breach when diplomacy falters and war threatens to consume all. They are not diplomats, and they are not soldiers. They operate in a realm that few can understand, using tools of influence and subterfuge to navigate the murky waters of international conflict.

To the public, these operatives are often invisible. They slip in and out of history, known only by code names and whispered rumors, leaving no trace behind. They are not the heroes who return to parades and accolades; they are the quiet warriors whose victories are celebrated only in silence. Yet it is through their actions that the world is kept from the brink of catastrophe. Their work is fraught with danger, as they confront not only hostile powers but the ever-present risk of exposure and betrayal. For them, success means the avoidance of conflict, the preservation of lives, and the maintenance of a precarious balance that keeps nations from tearing each other apart.

In the darkest hours of the Cold War, for instance, these secret heroes played a critical role. When open confrontation could have led to nuclear annihilation, it was the quiet maneuvers of spies and covert operatives that kept the fragile peace. They gathered intelligence, influenced foreign leaders, and used every means at their disposal to prevent the escalation of tensions. The Cuban Missile Crisis stands as a testament to their quiet heroism; while the world held its breath, covert operatives worked tirelessly behind the scenes to guide their nations through one of the most perilous moments in modern history.

Covert action is often misunderstood, painted as a world of intrigue and betrayal, but in reality, it is a tool of preservation. It allows nations to shape events without the destructive force of war, achieving outcomes that protect lives and maintain stability. In a world where open conflict remains all too common, covert action provides a way forward that spares the innocent and avoids the bloodshed that defines so much of human history. It is the option chosen when diplomacy has exhausted its potential, when negotiations have stalled, and when military force would bring devastation.

But covert action demands a certain kind of person—a rare breed who can operate in the shadows, driven by a sense of duty rather than personal gain. These operatives are bound by secrecy, often isolated from the very society they protect. They work in silence, knowing that their successes will go unrecognized and that their failures could mean death or disgrace. And yet they continue, fueled by the belief that their work makes a difference, that through their efforts, wars can be averted, and peace can be secured.

For those of us who value peace, these covert operatives are the unsung heroes. They walk a path fraught with danger, balancing on the edge between diplomacy and war. They are not idealists who believe in the inherent goodness of humanity; rather, they understand the harsh realities of power and the brutal calculus of survival. Yet, within that understanding lies a commitment to preserve life, to protect nations, and to prevent the horrors of war whenever possible.

In the chapters that follow, we will explore some of the pivotal moments in history where covert action saved lives and steered the world away from catastrophe. These are stories of deception and influence, of bravery and sacrifice, and above all, of the quiet heroes who dedicate their lives to peace in a world defined by conflict. Through their actions, they have left an indelible mark on history, proving time and again that peace can be won, not through the clash of armies, but through the calculated moves of operatives working in the shadows.

In a world shaped by violence, these operatives offer a glimpse of a different path, a path where wars are averted before they even begin, and where peace can be achieved, not by idealism, but by resolve and quiet determination. They are the true guardians of peace, the invisible hands that hold the world together when it threatens to fall apart. For all of human history, war has been the rule; through covert action, these operatives have shown us that peace—though elusive—is indeed possible.

Chapter 1: Roman Deception

The Gallic tribes were fierce, proud, and independent, their lands stretching from the mist-shrouded forests of Germania to the fertile plains of Gaul. United, they might have posed an existential threat to Rome's expansion. Yet, Julius Caesar, the ambitious Roman general, knew this strength was also their greatest vulnerability. Divided, the tribes were weaker—warlike, competitive, and often embroiled in disputes. Caesar saw in their rivalry a golden opportunity.

Caesar's campaign in Gaul was not only a march of legions but also a masterful display of psychological warfare and intelligence gathering. He knew that conquering Gaul by brute force would drain Rome's resources and stretch his forces thin. Instead, he relied on a mix of espionage, diplomatic manipulation, and carefully planted misinformation to ensure that the tribes would never unify.

Caesar had with him men known as speculatores, or scouts, and exploratores, who moved ahead of the legions, gathering information on terrain, troop movements, and the disposition of the Gallic tribes. These scouts slipped into villages under the guise of travelers or traders, listening to rumors, assessing allegiances, and bringing valuable intelligence back to their general. Through their work, Caesar built a detailed understanding of the alliances and tensions between the tribes.

Among the tribes, the most formidable was the Aedui, a powerful Gallic tribe often at odds with their neighbors, the Sequani. In previous years, the Sequani had sought aid from the Germanic warlord Ariovistus to secure dominance over the Aedui, inadvertently inviting a new threat into Gaul. Caesar saw an opening here. He carefully positioned himself as a protector of the Aedui, casting the Romans as allies in defense of Gallic autonomy against the foreign Germanic threat. The Aedui, seeing Rome as a counterbalance to their Germanic rivals, accepted the alliance.

But Caesar's true objective was more subtle. By aligning with the Aedui, he drove a wedge between them and other tribes, especially the Sequani. He presented himself as a friend to Gaul while quietly sowing distrust and division. To keep them from forming alliances against him, Caesar sent emissaries to various Gallic leaders, offering them promises of protection, supplies, and political support in exchange for their loyalty—or at least their neutrality.

The result was a network of alliances that kept the Gallic tribes fragmented. When one tribe showed signs of organizing resistance, Caesar would approach their rivals with promises of protection or support, further splintering any possibility of a unified front. His strategy created an environment of suspicion and prevented any one leader from rallying enough support to challenge Rome effectively.

The stakes rose dramatically when Vercingetorix, a charismatic young leader of the Arverni tribe, emerged as a unifying figure among the Gauls. Vercingetorix called upon his fellow tribes to resist Roman encroachment, and his appeal struck a chord across Gaul. His determination was a direct threat to Caesar's strategy; for the first time, there was a real possibility that the tribes might put aside their rivalries to confront a common enemy.

Caesar responded with his usual cunning. While his legions prepared for battle, his agents spread rumors among the tribes that Vercingetorix was only using them to consolidate his own power. They whispered that he sought to rule all Gaul, a claim that stirred resentment among proud chieftains who valued their independence. Caesar also took advantage of Vercingetorix's harsh tactics—punishing villages that did not join his rebellion—to paint him as a tyrant who would turn against his own people.

The rumors took hold, and support for Vercingetorix began to waver. Though he succeeded in uniting many tribes, others hesitated, distrustful of his motives and fearful of his ambition. Caesar's intelligence network fed him updates, allowing him to adapt his tactics, keeping Vercingetorix isolated and vulnerable.

The two forces met In a brutal siege at Alesia, a fortified hilltop settlement where Vercingetorix and his forces made their stand. Caesar's legions surrounded Alesia, constructing massive fortifications to prevent reinforcements from reaching the defenders. Meanwhile, he sent spies to disrupt communication and ensure that no other Gallic forces would come to Vercingetorix's aid.

After weeks of intense siege, Vercingetorix's forces, cut off and starving, finally surrendered. The Gallic resistance crumbled, and with it, any hope of a unified rebellion against Rome. Caesar's strategy of divide and conquer had succeeded not only through military might but also through a calculated campaign of psychological manipulation and espionage.

By the time the Gallic Wars ended, Caesar had effectively pacified Gaul, incorporating it into the Roman Republic. His victory was not merely the result of his legions' strength but also of his relentless intelligence operations and shrewd manipulation of tribal rivalries. Caesar returned to Rome not just as a conqueror but as a tactician who had wielded the power of deception as skillfully as any weapon.

The story of Julius Caesar in Gaul is a testament to the power of covert action and intelligence as tools of conquest and control. Through his agents and his mastery of psychological warfare, Caesar maintained a peace of sorts—a peace imposed through division, suspicion, and carefully crafted alliances. The tribes of Gaul, though subdued, had been spared the destruction of full-scale war through a strategy of espionage that was as invisible as it was effective. Caesar's legacy would echo through the ages, and his methods would be studied by generals and strategists for centuries to come.

Chapter 2: Shadows on the Silk Road

The Silk Road sprawled across Asia like a spider's web, connecting the heart of China to distant lands, and it carried not only silk and spices but also the future of the Han Dynasty. The Han Emperor, Wu, knew this better than anyone. If the road could remain open, the riches and influence it brought would bolster his empire's strength. Yet, beyond China's western borders, hostile tribes like the Xiongnu threatened this route. The Emperor needed alliances, friends in distant places who could help him hold these fierce enemies at bay. And for this task, he turned to Zhang Qian.

Zhang Qian was not a soldier nor a trader; he was a diplomat, chosen for his resilience and intelligence. His mission was not a conquest but a quest for peace. Emperor Wu sent Zhang westward to find the Yuezhi, a powerful tribe that had also suffered under the Xiongnu, in hopes of securing an alliance. This was the essence of early Chinese espionage—a mission born from necessity and aimed at averting the need for war.

Zhang knew the risks. The journey would take him through dangerous lands patrolled by Xiongnu raiders, who viewed anyone from Han territory as a threat. With a small party of men, Zhang set out, carrying gifts and letters as tokens of peace. The terrain was harsh, the heat merciless, and the threat of capture loomed at every turn. It was not long before Zhang's fears were realized—the Xiongnu caught him, and for over a decade, Zhang was held captive.

Yet, Zhang was patient. He learned their language, their ways, and bided his time. Finally, he saw an opportunity to escape, and with a few loyal companions, he fled under cover of night, trekking westward once more. He crossed mountains, rivers, and deserts, and after years of hardship, he reached the land of the Yuezhi.

The Yuezhi welcomed him, intrigued by his story and the gifts he brought. Zhang spoke of peace and cooperation, painting a vision of a prosperous Silk Road where their two peoples could benefit without bloodshed. The Yuezhi, however, had settled comfortably in their new lands and were wary of reigniting conflicts with the Xiongnu. Though Zhang failed to secure a formal alliance, his journey was far from wasted.

On his return to China, Zhang took a different route, stopping in other lands where he gathered valuable information about distant cultures, armies, and resources. He noted the agriculture of Fergana, the horses of Dayuan, and the wealth of Bactria, realizing that these places could become allies or trading partners for the Han Dynasty. He returned not with armies but with intelligence—a treasure as valuable as any military victory.

Emperor Wu welcomed Zhang back as a hero. The knowledge he brought back opened the Emperor's eyes to a world beyond China's borders, revealing allies and trade opportunities that had been mere legends. Emperor Wu wasted no time in acting on Zhang's intelligence. He forged trade agreements and established diplomatic relationships that allowed the Han Dynasty to expand its influence without bloodshed. The Silk Road flourished, and the wealth it brought strengthened the empire, while the alliances Zhang inspired kept potential enemies at bay.

Through diplomacy, espionage, and perseverance, Zhang Qian protected the Silk Road, securing a future for the Han Dynasty without ever lifting a sword. His journey became the foundation of Chinese foreign policy and intelligence, a testament to the power of quiet action and the subtle art of peace.

Chapter 3: The Spy Queen

The England of Queen Elizabeth I was a land fraught with danger, a Protestant island surrounded by Catholic powers that viewed her rule as illegitimate. Elizabeth's half-sister, Mary I, had brought England back under Catholicism, but Elizabeth reversed her policies, restoring Protestantism as the state religion. This move earned her the enmity of powerful figures across Europe, particularly King Philip II of Spain and the Pope, both of whom saw Elizabeth as a heretic and a threat to Catholic dominance. With rumors of plots swirling around the court and papal edicts calling for Elizabeth's overthrow, the need for security was paramount.

Enter Sir Francis Walsingham, Elizabeth's Secretary of State and chief spymaster. Walsingham was a devout Protestant who viewed the Catholic powers as existential threats to England and Elizabeth's rule. He was meticulous, calculating, and ruthless when it came to protecting his queen. Walsingham understood that England, outmatched militarily by Spain and France, could not rely on force alone. Instead, he would build an extensive network of spies across Europe, one of the earliest known intelligence networks, to identify and dismantle threats before they reached English soil.

Walsingham's network stretched across England and into the heart of Catholic Europe. His agents posed as diplomats, merchants, and even devout Catholics, gathering information and reporting back to him in coded messages. Walsingham knew that many Catholics within England considered Elizabeth's cousin, Mary, Queen of Scots, to be the legitimate ruler. Mary, a Catholic and former queen of France, had fled to England seeking Elizabeth's protection after being deposed in Scotland, but her presence only added fuel to the fire. Catholic plotters both inside and outside England viewed Mary as a viable alternative to Elizabeth.

Walsingham's suspicions grew when he learned of a conspiracy brewing among English Catholics and foreign allies to place Mary on the throne. This plot would become known as the Ridolfi Plot, named after Roberto Ridolfi, an Italian banker who conspired with the Duke of Norfolk and Spanish diplomats to assassinate Elizabeth. Their plan was to incite an uprising, assassinate Elizabeth, and install Mary as queen, backed by a Spanish invasion force. Walsingham's agents intercepted letters and uncovered the plot, and with this intelligence, he persuaded Elizabeth to execute the Duke of Norfolk, dismantling the conspiracy before it could materialize.

Walsingham knew, however, that the Ridolfi Plot was only the beginning. His network continued to gather intelligence on both Catholic and Protestant enemies, unraveling plots that sought to destabilize England. But the most infamous plot Walsingham foiled would come years later, in the form of the Babington Plot—a conspiracy that would lead to the downfall of Mary, Queen of Scots.

By 1586, Mary had been imprisoned for nearly two decades under suspicion of colluding with Catholic powers to overthrow Elizabeth. Despite her confinement, Mary continued to correspond with Catholic sympathizers, hoping for an opportunity to seize the throne. Walsingham, always one step ahead, devised a plan to expose Mary's involvement in a new plot to assassinate Elizabeth.

Using double agents and a carefully orchestrated trap, Walsingham had Mary's letters smuggled out of her prison, routed through his agents who controlled the correspondence. These letters were sent to a group of conspirators led by Anthony Babington, a young English Catholic who dreamed of freeing Mary and restoring Catholic rule. Babington and his co-conspirators wrote to Mary, pledging their support and detailing their plans to assassinate Elizabeth. Mary, seeing an opportunity, responded with her blessing, unaware that Walsingham's agents intercepted every letter.

Walsingham's trap was meticulous. Once he had sufficient evidence of Mary's involvement, he revealed the intercepted letters to Elizabeth's Privy Council. The contents of Mary's letters sealed her fate, showing her explicit support for Elizabeth's assassination. Walsingham's intelligence network had exposed a conspiracy that could have plunged England into chaos and led to a brutal invasion by Catholic forces. Mary was put on trial, convicted of treason, and executed in 1587.

Mary's death did not mark the end of Catholic threats to Elizabeth's reign. Walsingham's network continued to monitor threats from Spain, particularly as tensions between England and Spain escalated. In 1588, Philip II of Spain launched the Spanish Armada, intending to invade England and depose Elizabeth. Walsingham's network had provided advance warning of the Armada's mobilization, allowing the English navy to prepare its defenses. The Spanish Armada ultimately failed, repelled by England's superior naval tactics and unfavorable weather. Walsingham's intelligence network, though not directly responsible for the Armada's defeat, had given England the forewarning it needed.

In London, Walsingham's agents worked tirelessly to track down those who would support Catholic plots. They penetrated secret Catholic circles and sometimes posed as sympathizers to extract information, passing it back to Walsingham in code. The climate of suspicion and mistrust they fostered in Catholic networks was effective; every plotter knew that betrayal could be one spy away.

Through his dedication and ruthless efficiency, Walsingham's network preserved Elizabeth's rule and protected England from foreign threats. He was one of the earliest architects of modern intelligence, showing that espionage and covert action could be as powerful as armies in defending a nation. His legacy would shape the future of espionage, setting a precedent for the intelligence networks that would follow.

Elizabeth, who trusted few people completely, relied on Walsingham to be her eyes and ears in a hostile world. Through his intelligence network, Walsingham secured a precarious peace, deterring Catholic plots and thwarting invasions. The price of this peace was high—executions, betrayals, and an ever-present atmosphere of suspicion. But through Walsingham's efforts, England remained stable, and Elizabeth's reign endured as one of the most iconic in British history.

Chapter 4: Delphic Deceptions

The Peloponnesian War brought Greece to the edge of ruin.

City-states that had once flourished now lay devastated, as

Athens and Sparta dragged their allies into nearly three

decades of fierce, unrelenting struggle. Yet amid this violence,

certain figures worked tirelessly behind the scenes to prevent

conflict from escalating further, relying on cunning rather than

swords.

One of these figures was the Athenian general and statesman

Nicias. Known as a cautious and pragmatic leader, Nicias was

well aware that another major confrontation could mean

devastation for both Athens and Sparta. As the conflict wore

on, Nicias recognized that diplomacy, combined with well-

placed intelligence, could be a means to achieve a fragile

peace.

In the early stages of the war, both Athens and Sparta had

forces stationed across strategic points in Greece, with critical

tensions centered around the city of Delium. This location was not only a fortified city, but it was also close to Boeotia, a region pivotal to the balance of power. If Athens could control Boeotia, it could dominate central Greece, but if Sparta or its allies held it, Athens would be cut off from essential supplies and allies. Both sides knew this, and thus Delium became a point of contention.

Nicias understood the importance of preventing a direct clash over Delium and sought ways to secure Athens' position through intelligence rather than force. For this, he relied on a covert network of informants stationed in nearby cities and, most crucially, in Delphi. Delphi was a city that attracted travelers from all over Greece, including dignitaries from both Athens and Sparta. It was here, through a network of trusted priests and traders, that Nicias gathered information about the movements and intentions of Spartan forces and their allies.

One informant, a Boeotian merchant who regularly traveled between Athens, Sparta, and Delphi, was particularly valuable. He was able to move freely across borders, blending in among traders while quietly observing the military activity in both camps. His reports, passed in coded messages to Nicias' network, detailed Spartan troop numbers and possible routes they might use to reach Delium. These messages alerted Nicias that the Spartans were considering an attempt to capture Delium, which could lead to a full-scale confrontation.

With this intelligence in hand, Nicias devised a two-fold strategy to prevent the impending clash. First, he quietly fortified Delium, reinforcing the city's defenses and ensuring that it was well supplied. But Nicias knew that military preparations alone would not be enough to stave off an invasion; he needed to dissuade the Spartans from attacking entirely.

Nicias turned to his diplomatic network in Delphi, using intermediaries to open discreet communication with key Spartan leaders. Through indirect negotiations, he emphasized the costly consequences of another large-scale battle. He hinted at Athens' willingness to consider terms that could reduce tensions over the contested city. His approach was careful and subtle, designed not to reveal weakness but to suggest that both sides had more to gain from restraint than from outright conflict.

At the same time, Nicias used disinformation as a tool to reinforce his message. His operatives spread rumors within Spartan ranks that Athens was prepared to bring in reinforcements from its allies in Ionia, should Sparta push for an invasion. This strategic misinformation created uncertainty, making the Spartan leaders reconsider the cost of advancing into Delium.

As Nicias' network spread these rumors, his diplomatic overtures gained traction. Spartan commanders, receiving conflicting reports about Athenian strength, began to doubt the wisdom of launching an assault on Delium. Faced with uncertain intelligence and wary of a potential ambush, they opted to halt their advance. For a brief moment, Nicias' efforts had prevented another escalation, securing a temporary peace in Boeotia.

Despite the ongoing conflict elsewhere, the situation at Delium remained stable. Nicias' blend of intelligence, diplomacy, and misdirection bought Athens the time it needed to strengthen its defenses and prevented Sparta from seizing a strategic position that could have worsened the war for both sides. His quiet efforts in the background showed that sometimes, peace could be achieved not through overt shows of force, but through silent and calculated actions.

Though the Peloponnesian War would drag on for years, Nicias' work as a cautious strategist left an indelible mark. His belief in the power of intelligence and diplomacy over battle set him apart from other Athenian leaders of his time. In an era when Athens was known for its bold, often reckless ambitions, Nicias represented a different path—one that acknowledged the limits of warfare and the necessity of preventing conflict wherever possible.

Nicias' legacy would come to be defined not by victory in battle, but by his commitment to peace, even amid one of history's longest and most devastating wars. His intelligence efforts, though unsung by the chroniclers of his age, quietly influenced the course of the Peloponnesian War, proving that even in times of violence, there are those who work for peace in the shadows.

Chapter 5: The Cardinal

France in the early 17th century was a fragile kingdom surrounded by hostile powers and deeply divided internally. Religious and political rivalries threatened to tear the nation apart, and on its borders, rival kingdoms like Spain and the Holy Roman Empire waited for a chance to strike. At the heart of French politics was Cardinal Richelieu, chief minister to King Louis XIII, a shrewd and calculating statesman determined to protect France's interests. Richelieu understood that direct conflict could lead to disaster, given France's vulnerable position. Instead, he would use intelligence and manipulation to protect the kingdom and maintain its balance of power in Europe.

Richelieu's primary goal was to prevent France from being drawn into the bloody wars that had engulfed the rest of Europe, particularly the Thirty Years' War. The conflict, which had started in 1618, ravaged Central Europe, pitting Protestant and Catholic states against each other in a brutal struggle that devastated entire regions. France, although a Catholic country, faced threats from both Catholic Spain and the Holy Roman Empire, both of which sought to curtail French influence. Richelieu saw an opportunity to weaken these powers through covert means, keeping France out of direct conflict while ensuring that its rivals would be too preoccupied with their own struggles to focus on France.

To this end, Richelieu built a network of spies and agents, a web of mirrors that extended across Europe. His agents were embedded in courts, taverns, and religious institutions, working under false identities to gather intelligence and spread disinformation. Richelieu's operatives served a dual purpose: they provided him with crucial intelligence on the movements and intentions of hostile powers, and they sowed discord within enemy ranks, destabilizing alliances that could threaten France.

One of Richelieu's most trusted agents was Father Joseph, a Capuchin monk known as "the Grey Eminence" due to his close relationship with the Cardinal and his unassuming appearance. Father Joseph was a master of manipulation and used his position as a priest to gain access to influential figures across Europe. Disguised as a humble clergyman, he traveled under the guise of religious pilgrimage, collecting valuable intelligence and passing it back to Richelieu. Father Joseph's reports were filled with details about political tensions, military plans, and potential alliances, providing Richelieu with the information he needed to stay one step ahead of his enemies.

One of Richelieu's greatest successes was his manipulation of the German Protestant princes within the Holy Roman Empire. While Richelieu was a Catholic, he recognized that supporting the Protestant princes against the Catholic Habsburgs, who ruled the Holy Roman Empire, would serve France's interests by keeping the Empire divided. Richelieu covertly funneled funds and arms to Protestant leaders like Gustavus Adolphus of Sweden, who was actively fighting the Habsburgs. By supporting Protestant forces, Richelieu kept the Empire embroiled in internal conflict, ensuring that its resources and attention were focused inward rather than on expanding against France.

Richelieu's intelligence network also extended into Spain, where his agents fed disinformation and carefully crafted rumors designed to stoke tensions between Spain and the Habsburgs. Richelieu's spies in Madrid reported that Spanish nobility harbored growing resentment toward the Habsburg rulers, particularly regarding their involvement in costly foreign wars. Richelieu seized on these tensions, using his agents to subtly encourage Spanish nobles to question the wisdom of further entanglement in European conflicts. By fostering a climate of dissent within Spain, Richelieu effectively limited Spain's willingness to commit fully to the Catholic cause in the Thirty Years' War.

In addition to keeping Spain occupied, Richelieu employed his agents to disrupt potential alliances against France within the Italian states. Italy, a patchwork of city-states and principalities, was a hotspot for European power struggles. The Duke of Savoy, an influential Italian leader, had at various times shown both anti-French and pro-Spanish inclinations, making him a volatile figure in Richelieu's calculations. Recognizing the Duke's ambitions, Richelieu's operatives planted rumors suggesting that Spain planned to undermine the Duke's authority, subtly nudging him toward a neutral stance or even a tentative alliance with France.

Meanwhile, Richelieu paid close attention to England, where civil and religious tensions simmered beneath the surface. Through diplomatic and covert channels, Richelieu encouraged factions within the English court to oppose any potential alliance with Spain or the Holy Roman Empire. In particular, Richelieu worked to influence members of Parliament who were critical of King Charles I's foreign policy, sowing seeds of doubt about the value of siding with Catholic powers. His efforts contributed to a political climate in England that made it increasingly difficult for Charles to pursue any strong anti-French alignment.

One of the Cardinal's boldest covert actions involved his network's use of disinformation to prevent a joint attack by Spain and the Holy Roman Empire on French territories in the Pyrenees. Through carefully planted rumors, Richelieu's agents convinced the Spanish commanders that French forces in the region were far stronger and more prepared than they actually were. Additionally, the operatives spread exaggerated reports of local rebellions within Spanish territories, leading the Spanish crown to recall troops that had been intended for the invasion. By manipulating the perception of France's strength and internal threats in Spain, Richelieu averted a potentially catastrophic conflict.

Through his web of spies and his deft manipulation of European politics, Richelieu succeeded in preventing France from being drawn into a large-scale war. His policies allowed France to emerge from the Thirty Years' War as a dominant power, with its rivals weakened by years of continuous fighting. Richelieu's legacy as a master strategist lay in his understanding that a kingdom's greatest defense was often its ability to navigate the shadows of diplomacy and espionage rather than relying solely on military force.

Richelieu's network exemplified the power of statecraft and covert action as tools of peace. By destabilizing France's enemies, he kept them entangled in their own problems, preventing any unified force from rising against France. His approach minimized the need for open conflict, allowing France to strengthen itself without being drawn into costly battles.

For Cardinal Richelieu, the path to peace was not through treaties or negotiations alone but through an intricate web of deception, disinformation, and diplomacy. He used covert action to reshape the balance of power in Europe, ensuring that France would not just survive but emerge as a leading force. His legacy as the master of France's "Web of Mirrors" endures as a testament to the quiet victories of intelligence and manipulation in the quest for stability.

Chapter 6: Quite Diplomacy

By 1814, the War of 1812 had dragged on for two exhausting years. The United States and Britain found themselves locked in a brutal conflict that stretched from the shores of the Atlantic to the Great Lakes. Yet, neither side had achieved a decisive victory, and both were weary. Britain, preoccupied with the ongoing Napoleonic Wars, had limited resources for a prolonged fight across the Atlantic. The United States, still a young nation, was stretched thin, with its ports blockaded and its capital, Washington D.C., recently burned by British forces. Behind the scenes, diplomatic efforts were quietly underway to bring the war to a close before it escalated into a more devastating conflict.

President James Madison recognized that the war's continuation threatened the survival of the American republic. British forces had seized control of swathes of American territory, and with no allies in Europe, the United States faced the prospect of fighting alone against the world's most powerful navy. Britain, too, was feeling the strain. With Napoleon's defeat seeming imminent, British leaders worried that prolonged hostilities with America could weaken their strategic position, especially if another European power decided to intervene. Quietly, both sides began searching for a way to end the war.

The path to peace lay not In open diplomacy but in the skillful and covert efforts of intermediaries who bridged the Atlantic divide. One of the key figures in these back-channel efforts was Albert Gallatin, a Swiss-American statesman and Madison's Secretary of the Treasury. Gallatin, well-versed in European politics and fluent in French, was dispatched to Europe to engage in secret negotiations, traveling under the pretense of managing U.S. finances abroad. Gallatin's quiet diplomacy would prove instrumental in bringing the warring nations to the negotiating table.

While Gallatin operated from Europe, other American diplomats, including John Quincy Adams, were stationed in neutral Ghent (now in Belgium), where informal meetings with British representatives could take place away from public scrutiny. The choice of Ghent as a location for these covert discussions was no accident; it was a city outside the sphere of influence of the major European powers, offering a safe and neutral ground. Both sides agreed to keep their negotiations confidential to avoid alarming their allies or emboldening their enemies.

At the same time, back-channel messages between London and Washington were exchanged via intermediaries, diplomats who traveled in secrecy between the British Foreign Office and the American delegation. These couriers passed carefully worded messages, each side testing the other's willingness to compromise without giving away too much. The messages were often conveyed through trusted merchants and private citizens, maintaining a layer of deniability.

Gallatin and Adams knew that the British would not concede easily, especially given their military advantage. To prevent a breakdown in talks, they skillfully used a mix of strategic concessions and subtle threats. Gallatin suggested to British diplomats that the United States could consider relinquishing claims to Canada, thereby giving Britain control over valuable territory. However, he also hinted that prolonging the war might lead America to strengthen ties with other European powers, potentially challenging Britain's dominance in North America.

Gallatin and Adams understood that these indirect messages played into British fears. Britain's leaders were wary of France, even with Napoleon seemingly defeated. The idea of America aligning more closely with another European power was unsettling, especially as it would mean a continued drain on Britain's resources. To further pressure the British, Gallatin worked quietly with European merchants to spread the word that America might consider reopening trade routes with nations that opposed Britain if peace was not achieved. This tactic sent a signal that the United States could weather the economic hardships, however painful, and hold out for favorable terms.

In parallel, the British diplomats received covert reports that their own citizens, weary of the war's cost, were increasingly resistant to continued conflict across the ocean. These reports, often gathered by British spies and traders in American ports, revealed a growing resentment in American society toward the war, which British leaders interpreted as an opportunity to secure favorable terms. However, Gallatin's covert influence with European allies suggested that American resilience was stronger than appearances suggested, and his subtle diplomatic maneuvers kept the British guessing.

The stakes grew even higher in 1814, as the British prepared for a decisive invasion along the eastern coast of the United States, aiming to bring the Americans to their knees. News of this plan reached Gallatin through informal channels, prompting him to intensify his efforts to bring about peace before the British invasion could materialize. He appealed to British diplomats, emphasizing the humanitarian costs of continuing the conflict and the economic benefits of restoring peace. Gallatin's arguments began to resonate as British diplomats weighed the advantages of a stable North America against the risk of a prolonged, costly occupation.

Finally, after months of back-channel negotiations, a breakthrough emerged. Both sides agreed to meet in Ghent in earnest, sending full delegations to hammer out the details of a peace treaty. The negotiations were tense, each side reluctant to concede too much. The Americans wanted assurances that British forces would withdraw from occupied territories, while the British sought to protect their commercial interests and prevent American expansion into indigenous lands.

Over weeks of closed-door meetings, Gallatin and Adams, along with British representatives, carefully crafted the terms of peace. Gallatin's quiet diplomacy and steady influence helped both sides to find middle ground. Ultimately, the Treaty of Ghent was signed on December 24, 1814, bringing an official end to hostilities without either side claiming victory. The treaty restored the pre-war boundaries, ensuring that neither nation would gain or lose territory—a compromise that allowed both countries to save face.

Thanks to Gallatin's covert efforts and back-channel diplomacy, the Treaty of Ghent prevented the escalation of a war that could have devastated both nations. Without Gallatin's quiet influence, the War of 1812 might have dragged on, leaving America weakened and susceptible to further conflicts with European powers. Instead, his work helped secure a peace that allowed the young United States to focus on internal development and westward expansion.

The Treaty of Ghent, though celebrated quietly at the time, became a landmark in American history. Through skillful diplomacy and covert negotiations, Gallatin, Adams, and their allies had navigated a path to peace that spared the United States further suffering and strengthened its position in the international arena. Their work is a testament to the power of quiet negotiation, proving that the greatest victories are those that avoid battle altogether.

Chapter 7: The Secrets of the Pharaoh

Beneath the grandeur of pyramids and the enigmatic gaze of the Sphinx lay a web of intrigue that secured Egypt's power and stability for centuries. Espionage wasn't just a modern invention; its roots trace back to the fertile lands of the Nile, where pharaohs wielded covert intelligence as a vital weapon in their arsenal of statecraft. In this chapter, we delve into the clandestine world of spies and informants who served the Egyptian empire, manipulating rival city-states, uncovering plots, and ensuring the security of Egypt's borders.

The pharaohs of ancient Egypt were not merely rulers; they were divine figures tasked with preserving maat—the harmony and order of the universe. Maintaining this cosmic balance required more than religious rituals and military might; it demanded strategic intelligence. The pharaoh's spies, often drawn from scribes, merchants, and even priests, infiltrated foreign courts, eavesdropped in bustling marketplaces, and fed vital information back to the royal court. These operatives were the unseen hands guiding Egypt's diplomacy and military strategies.

One of the most striking examples of Egyptian espionage was their use of double agents and disinformation campaigns to destabilize rival city-states. Letters unearthed in the Amarna archives reveal how Egyptian emissaries spread false information to sow discord among enemy alliances, preventing invasions before they could be mounted. The pharaohs' operatives also gathered intelligence on troop movements, trade routes, and political unrest, enabling Egypt to strike preemptively or negotiate from a position of strength.

The art of espionage extended beyond foreign affairs. Domestically, the pharaoh's network of spies monitored potential dissent among nobles and priests. Temples, often centers of wealth and influence, were closely watched for signs of rebellion. Priests, who wielded significant power in interpreting the gods' will, were both a resource and a threat, necessitating careful surveillance. This intelligence network ensured that the pharaoh maintained control not just over the land but over the hearts and minds of the people.

Espionage in ancient Egypt wasn't solely about survival; it was about preserving legacy. The pharaohs understood that intelligence was the key to securing not just their reign but the enduring power of their civilization. Their use of espionage laid the groundwork for statecraft practices that would echo through history, influencing empires to come.

Through the shadows cast by towering monuments, the pharaohs' spies wove a narrative of intrigue and strategy that allowed Egypt to flourish for millennia. As we peel back the layers of history, we uncover the timeless truth: intelligence and strategy have always been as crucial to leadership as the sword and the scepter.

Chapter 8: Shadows of the Rising Sun

Feudal Japan during the Tokugawa Shogunate was a land of swords, honor, and whispered secrets. Beneath the surface of its rigid societal order and the serene beauty of its temples and gardens lay a hidden network of operatives who ensured the fragile unity of the nation. The Tokugawa shoguns, determined to maintain peace after centuries of civil war, turned to the shadowy world of ninja operatives. This chapter delves into how these covert agents wielded deception, manipulation, and intelligence to hold a fractious Japan together.

The Tokugawa period, also known as the Edo period, was marked by an uneasy peace. The shogunate's rule depended on balancing the power of warring clans, ensuring no single daimyo gained enough strength to challenge the central authority. To maintain this delicate equilibrium, the shoguns deployed ninja networks—highly skilled operatives trained in espionage, sabotage, and subterfuge. Unlike the romanticized assassins of legend, these ninjas were masters of stealth and intelligence, operating invisibly to manipulate the feudal chessboard.

Ninja operatives infiltrated rival clans, gathering crucial information on troop movements, alliances, and plots. By cultivating informants within enemy ranks, they could feed misinformation to foment discord and mistrust. For instance, a ninja might intercept and alter correspondence between clans, creating the illusion of betrayal and fracturing alliances before they could threaten the shogunate's stability. These subtle acts of sabotage were often more effective than direct confrontation, ensuring that battles were avoided before swords were drawn.

The ninja's role extended beyond spying. They were experts in psychological warfare, leveraging rumors and symbols to sow fear or project power. A well-placed emblem of the shogunate or a cryptic message left at a daimyo's stronghold could create paranoia, leading rivals to overestimate the shogunate's reach and strength. These operatives used deception as a weapon, ensuring loyalty through fear and uncertainty rather than open force.

The Iga and Kōga clans, renowned for their ninja traditions, were pivotal in the Tokugawa intelligence network. Their operatives were deployed to surveil and neutralize internal threats, from rebellious daimyos to unruly samurai. By keeping potential challengers under constant watch, the shogunate maintained its iron grip on power. These ninja networks operated in the shadows, ensuring that the surface calm of the Tokugawa era was preserved.

But the ninja's greatest strength was their anonymity. Unlike the samurai, who sought honor and recognition, the ninja thrived in obscurity. Their ability to blend into the fabric of feudal society made them the perfect tool for a shogunate that needed quiet control rather than open displays of power. They were the silent guardians of unity, preventing civil war through acts of calculated deception.

The Tokugawa Shogunate understood a timeless truth: the most effective power is often unseen. By mastering the arts of deception and intelligence, the shogunate secured two centuries of peace in Japan. This chapter reveals how the shadows cast by the ninja shaped the rising sun of Tokugawa rule and cemented espionage as an enduring tool of statecraft.

Chapter 9: Napoleon and the British Spies

By the early 19th century, Napoleon Bonaparte's empire stretched across much of Europe, and his ambition seemed boundless. Britain stood alone as a bulwark against his domination, its powerful navy ensuring that French forces could not easily cross the English Channel. However, the threat of invasion loomed large. Napoleon amassed troops at Boulogne, just across the channel, in what appeared to be the staging ground for a full-scale assault on Britain. The British government, led by Prime Minister William Pitt the Younger, knew they could not rely on military strength alone to thwart the French emperor's ambitions. It was time for the shadowy world of intelligence and disinformation to take center stage.

The British Secret Service, still in its infancy, became a crucial weapon in the fight against Napoleon. Britain's spymasters understood that Napoleon's strength lay not only in his military prowess but in his ability to inspire fear and loyalty among his troops and allies. To counter this, they turned to deception, creating a campaign designed to undermine Napoleon's confidence, sow discord among his allies, and misdirect his military efforts.

One of the most effective strategies employed by British intelligence was the use of disinformation to fuel Napoleon's paranoia. Spies and agents infiltrated Napoleon's court and military circles, posing as disgruntled officers, merchants, and even diplomats. These agents spread rumors of dissent within Napoleon's ranks, suggesting that some of his closest generals were secretly conspiring against him. These rumors, carefully tailored to play on Napoleon's insecurities, were designed to erode trust within the French command structure and distract the emperor from focusing on his invasion plans.

A particularly audacious piece of disinformation involved the creation of a false plot against Napoleon's life. British agents fabricated evidence of a conspiracy involving French royalists and exiled émigrés, claiming they had infiltrated Napoleon's inner circle. Fake documents, letters, and coded messages were strategically "leaked" to French intelligence, leading Napoleon to launch an internal investigation. The resulting witch hunt consumed valuable time and resources, disrupting his preparations for the invasion of Britain.

Meanwhile, the British used their naval dominance to project an image of overwhelming strength. Through intercepted communications and planted reports, British intelligence convinced Napoleon that the Royal Navy was prepared to blockade every French port and intercept any invasion fleet. These exaggerated claims, coupled with real naval maneuvers designed to be highly visible, forced Napoleon to reconsider the feasibility of his plans.

The British also targeted Napoleon's allies, particularly in Central Europe. Spies and diplomats spread false reports of

British alliances with various German states, hinting that uprisings against French rule were imminent. These efforts were aimed at keeping Napoleon's attention divided, forcing him to deploy troops to maintain control over his satellite states rather than concentrating them at Boulogne for the invasion. The British intelligence network even circulated rumors that Austria, still licking its wounds after its defeat at Austerlitz, was preparing to rejoin the fight against France.

One of the most significant acts of disinformation involved the so-called "phantom fleet." British intelligence fabricated reports that a large fleet of British ships was secretly stationed in the Baltic Sea, ready to strike French ports or intercept Napoleon's forces. These false reports reached Napoleon through double agents and intercepted correspondence, further convincing him that Britain's defenses were impenetrable. The phantom fleet never existed, but the mere belief in its presence caused Napoleon to redirect resources and delay his invasion plans.

Perhaps the most critical moment in Britain's campaign of disinformation came in 1805 when Napoleon abruptly shifted his focus from Britain to Central Europe. His decision to march his army eastward to confront the Third Coalition—an alliance of Britain, Austria, and Russia—was influenced, in part, by the carefully crafted narrative that Britain was unassailable. Napoleon abandoned his invasion plans and directed his forces toward Austria, leading to the famed Battle of Austerlitz. While Austerlitz was a resounding French victory, it marked the end of Napoleon's immediate threat to Britain.

The British intelligence campaign against Napoleon exemplified the art of disinformation. By playing on Napoleon's fears and manipulating his perceptions, British operatives altered the course of the conflict without engaging in direct combat. Their efforts not only protected Britain from invasion but also bought time for the Royal Navy to strengthen its defenses and for Britain to solidify its alliances across Europe.

Chapter 10: The Venetian Mask

Renaissance Italy was a mosaic of rival city-states, each vying for power, wealth, and influence. Among them, Venice stood apart. The Serene Republic, as it was called, was a maritime superpower with a vast trade empire stretching across the Mediterranean. Yet, its wealth and strategic location made it a prime target for ambitious neighbors like Milan, Florence, and the Papal States. In an age where diplomacy often gave way to violence, Venice relied on its greatest weapon: information.

Venice's Council of Ten, a secretive governing body, oversaw the city's intelligence operations. The council maintained an extensive network of spies, informants, and diplomats who operated across Europe and the Ottoman Empire. Venetian spies were masters of deception, trained to extract secrets, spread disinformation, and manipulate alliances. Their work was instrumental in protecting the Republic from threats and preserving its neutrality in a region perpetually on the brink of war.

In the late 15th century, Venice faced a grave threat. Ludovico Sforza, the Duke of Milan, had been consolidating power in northern Italy, building alliances that threatened Venice's position. Sforza's ambitions were no secret, but the exact nature of his plans remained unclear. The Council of Ten dispatched one of their most skilled operatives, known only by the codename "Il Corvo" (The Raven), to infiltrate Sforza's court and uncover his intentions.

Il Corvo's mission was perilous. Disguised as a merchant, he traveled to Milan, where he gained access to Sforza's inner circle by posing as a supplier of luxury goods. Venetian spies were trained not only in languages and codes but also in the subtle art of social manipulation. Il Corvo used flattery and charm to befriend key courtiers, carefully piecing together intelligence about Sforza's plans.

Over weeks of patient observation and covert conversations, Il Corvo uncovered a plot that could plunge northern Italy into war. Sforza had been negotiating a secret alliance with the King of France, Charles VIII, who sought to expand his influence into Italy. In exchange for French military support, Sforza promised to help Charles claim the Kingdom of Naples, a prize long contested by European powers. If successful, this alliance would destabilize the Italian states and threaten Venice's independence.

Il Corvo knew that direct confrontation with Sforza was not an option. Venice, though wealthy, lacked the military strength to counter a Franco-Milanese alliance. Instead, he turned to Venice's tried-and-true strategy: divide and manipulate. Through intermediaries, Il Corvo began spreading rumors among Milan's allies, suggesting that Sforza intended to betray them once his alliance with France was secure. These whispers sowed doubt and mistrust, weakening the unity of Sforza's coalition.

Simultaneously, Il Corvo sent coded messages back to the Council of Ten, detailing the Franco-Milanese negotiations. The council acted swiftly, deploying envoys to Florence and the Papal States, warning them of Sforza's ambitions and urging them to oppose the alliance. Venetian diplomats offered trade concessions and financial incentives to strengthen these ties, ensuring that Sforza would face resistance if he moved forward with his plans.

In a stroke of brilliance, Il Corvo also targeted Charles VIII's court. Through Venetian agents in France, he spread disinformation suggesting that Sforza was simultaneously negotiating with Ferdinand of Aragon, the King of Naples, to secure his favor in case the French alliance failed. This disinformation reached Charles, who began to question Sforza's loyalty and hesitated to commit fully to the alliance.

The combined efforts of Il Corvo and Venice's diplomats paid off. Sforza's plans unraveled as mistrust among his allies grew and French support wavered. Without a united front, Sforza abandoned his ambitions for a Franco-Milanese alliance. Venice, meanwhile, strengthened its position, securing peace with its neighbors through careful diplomacy and the strategic use of intelligence.

Il Corvo returned to Venice in secrecy, his mission complete.

The Council of Ten, ever vigilant, recorded his success in their

private archives, but his name would never be known. Like all

Venetian spies, his work remained in the shadows,

uncelebrated but vital to the Republic's survival

Chapter 11: Ottoman Intrigue

By the early 1850s, the Ottoman Empire was often called the

"Sick Man of Europe," a term reflecting its declining influence

in a world increasingly shaped by the ambitions of rising

European powers. Yet, the empire remained a key player in

global geopolitics, its strategic position bridging Europe, Asia,

and the Middle East. Nowhere was this more apparent than in

the Balkans, where Russia's expansionist ambitions

threatened to destabilize the region and challenge the

Ottoman Empire's sovereignty. Faced with mounting tensions

and the looming specter of war, the Ottomans turned to covert

diplomacy and strategic intelligence to avoid disaster.

The crisis began In 1853, when Tsar Nicholas I of Russia demanded that the Ottoman Empire grant him exclusive rights to protect Orthodox Christians within its territories. Though framed as a benevolent gesture, the demand was a thinly veiled power play, one that would have severely undermined Ottoman sovereignty. Sultan Abdülmecid I understood the stakes immediately. Agreeing to Russia's terms would set a dangerous precedent, effectively ceding control of the empire's internal affairs to a foreign power. Refusing, however, risked provoking a war that the Ottomans were ill-prepared to fight. It was a delicate situation, one that called for diplomacy conducted in the shadows.

Sultan Abdülmecid turned to one of his most trusted advisors, Mehmed Emin Ali Pasha, to navigate the crisis. Ali Pasha, the Ottoman Empire's Grand Vizier and chief diplomat, was a master of negotiation, known for his ability to balance competing interests and forge unlikely alliances. He recognized that the empire could not confront Russia alone; it needed the support of Britain, France, and Austria to counterbalance Russian aggression. However, these powers had their own interests in the region, and uniting them behind the Ottoman cause would require careful maneuvering.

Ali Pasha began by dispatching emissaries to London and Paris, using private channels to emphasize the threat posed by Russian expansion. He framed the crisis not as a local dispute but as a challenge to the broader European balance of power. By highlighting the strategic importance of the Eastern Mediterranean and the potential disruption of trade routes, Ali Pasha appealed to Britain and France's self-interest. Through subtle persuasion, he convinced them that supporting the Ottoman Empire was not merely an act of goodwill but a necessity to curb Russian ambitions.

Meanwhile, Ottoman operatives in the Balkans worked to undermine Russia's influence among the region's Orthodox Christian communities. These agents spread rumors that Russia's promises of protection were a guise for imperial domination, aimed at exploiting local populations for its own gain. By planting seeds of distrust, the Ottomans weakened

Russia's hold on key communities, making it harder for the tsar to justify his demands.

One of the most significant breakthroughs came when Ottoman agents intercepted intelligence indicating that Russia planned to mobilize troops in the Danubian Principalities of Moldavia and Wallachia. These regions, under nominal Ottoman suzerainty, were critical to the balance of power in the Balkans. Russian military action there would be a clear provocation, one that could escalate into full-scale war. Rather than respond with force, Ali Pasha used the intelligence to rally diplomatic support. He informed British and French diplomats of Russia's plans, urging them to pressure Austria to take a firm stance against Russian aggression. Austria, historically wary of Russian expansion, responded by reinforcing its borders and signaling its willingness to oppose unilateral Russian actions.

At the same time, Ali Pasha orchestrated a covert diplomatic initiative aimed at diffusing tensions with Russia. Through intermediaries, he proposed a compromise that would address some of Russia's concerns without ceding Ottoman sovereignty. The proposal included limited concessions, such as greater autonomy for Orthodox Christian communities, but fell short of granting Russia exclusive rights. These secret negotiations bought the Ottomans valuable time, delaying Russian action and keeping the possibility of peace alive.

However, Tsar Nicholas I, frustrated by the lack of progress, ordered Russian forces to occupy Moldavia and Wallachia in July 1853. The move escalated the crisis, prompting the Ottomans to declare war. Even as hostilities began, Ali Pasha continued to work behind the scenes to prevent the conflict from spiraling out of control. He instructed Ottoman agents in Europe to spread exaggerated reports of logistical difficulties within the Russian army and growing unrest in Russian-controlled territories. These disinformation campaigns created doubts about Russia's ability to sustain a prolonged conflict, further isolating the tsar diplomatically.

Ali Pasha also sought to strengthen the Ottoman Empire's position through alliances. He successfully persuaded Britain and France to formalize their support, transforming the conflict into a broader European issue. By framing the war as a defense of European stability against Russian aggression, Ali Pasha ensured that the Ottoman Empire would not stand alone. This strategic alignment culminated in the entry of British and French forces into the war in 1854, shifting the balance of power and preventing a unilateral Russian victory.

Despite the outbreak of the Crimean War, Ali Pasha's efforts in the preceding months had achieved a crucial objective: avoiding a direct and devastating conflict between the Ottoman Empire and Russia. His use of covert diplomacy and intelligence not only delayed Russian aggression but also ensured that the Ottomans entered the war with the backing of powerful allies. Without Ali Pasha's efforts, the war could have been far more catastrophic for the Ottoman Empire, potentially leading to the loss of its Balkan territories and further erosion of its sovereignty.

Chap 12: Falcon and the Shah

The Safavid Empire of Persia, flourishing between the 16th and 18th centuries, stood as a beacon of culture and power in a region fraught with volatility. Positioned between the Ottoman Empire to the west and the Mughal Empire to the east, Persia was constantly at risk of invasion. Safavid rulers, particularly Shah Abbas I, understood that survival required more than military might; it demanded cunning, diplomacy, and covert action. The Safavids developed an intricate network of spies and informants who operated in secrecy to gather intelligence and manipulate rivals, ensuring the empire's stability without plunging it into unnecessary wars.

Shah Abbas I, known as "The Great," reigned during the empire's zenith in the late 16th and early 17th centuries. A visionary leader, Abbas reformed Persia's military and administration while recognizing the power of intelligence in statecraft. His reign coincided with growing tensions between Persia and the Ottoman Empire, a rival not only in territorial ambition but also in religious identity, with the Safavids championing Shi'a Islam against the Sunni Ottomans. The

Safavids also faced threats from Central Asian tribes and internal unrest, requiring a deft balance of force and subterfuge.

Among Shah Abbas's most trusted operatives was a man known only by his code name, "The Falcon." Operating in the shadowy world of Safavid intelligence, The Falcon worked tirelessly to monitor the movements of Persia's enemies, uncover conspiracies, and disrupt plots before they could materialize. His mission was not only to protect the empire's borders but also to prevent the outbreak of conflicts that could strain Persia's resources and endanger its people.

One of The Falcon's most critical assignments came during a period of heightened tensions with the Ottomans. The two empires had clashed repeatedly over territories in the Caucasus, with both sides vying for control of key trade routes. In the early 1600s, intelligence reached Shah Abbas that the Ottomans were amassing troops near the border, possibly in preparation for an invasion. Rather than respond with force, Abbas dispatched The Falcon to infiltrate the Ottoman court and uncover the true extent of their plans.

Disguised as a merchant, The Falcon traveled to Istanbul, where he embedded himself in the bustling markets and vibrant social circles frequented by Ottoman officials. He used his cover to gather intelligence, befriending courtiers and traders who unwittingly provided valuable information about troop movements and political dynamics within the empire. Through careful observation and subtle questioning, The Falcon discovered that the Ottoman troop buildup was not an immediate threat but rather a display of power intended to intimidate Persia into making territorial concessions.

Armed with this knowledge, Shah Abbas devised a strategy to counter the Ottoman posturing without resorting to war. He instructed The Falcon to spread rumors within the Ottoman court that Persia had formed a secret alliance with the Crimean Khanate, a vassal state of the Ottomans. The fabricated alliance, though entirely false, suggested that any Ottoman aggression toward Persia would trigger a broader conflict, forcing the Ottomans to divide their forces. This disinformation campaign sowed doubt and caution among Ottoman leaders, delaying any plans for an invasion.

Meanwhile, Shah Abbas strengthened his diplomatic ties with European powers, particularly England and the Netherlands, who were eager to weaken Ottoman dominance in the region. Safavid envoys, armed with intelligence gathered by operatives like The Falcon, presented Persia as a stable and reliable ally against the Ottomans. These efforts not only secured critical trade agreements but also discouraged the Ottomans from escalating hostilities, knowing that Persia could potentially leverage European support.

The Falcon's work extended beyond espionage against external enemies. Within Persia, he monitored dissident factions and uncovered conspiracies that could destabilize the empire. In one notable instance, he intercepted a plot by a faction of rebellious nobles to align with the Uzbeks, a Central Asian power threatening Persia's northeastern borders. Acting swiftly, The Falcon relayed the details to Shah Abbas, who neutralized the threat through a combination of calculated concessions and decisive action against the conspirators. This prevented an internal uprising that could have left Persia vulnerable to external attacks.

Another critical moment in The Falcon's career came during negotiations with the Mughal Empire to the east. Relations between the Safavids and the Mughals were often tense, particularly over control of Kandahar, a strategically vital city on the frontier. Shah Abbas, aware that the Mughals were preoccupied with internal challenges, instructed The Falcon to gather intelligence on Mughal court dynamics and identify opportunities to de-escalate tensions. The Falcon's reports highlighted divisions within the Mughal leadership, which Shah Abbas used to propose a temporary non-aggression pact. This agreement allowed both empires to focus on their respective priorities without the distraction of conflict.

The Falcon's ability to operate in secrecy and his mastery of deception were vital to the Safavid Empire's success in navigating its complex geopolitical landscape. His intelligence gathering and disinformation campaigns averted multiple wars, preserving Persia's resources and enabling Shah Abbas to focus on strengthening the empire from within. Through espionage, the Safavids maintained a delicate balance of power, ensuring that their rivals remained cautious and divided.

Under Shah Abbas's leadership, Persia thrived as a center of art, culture, and commerce, its borders secure thanks to the unseen efforts of operatives like The Falcon. The Safavid intelligence network exemplified the power of espionage as a tool of statecraft, demonstrating that wars could often be avoided through cunning and foresight. By staying one step ahead of their enemies, the Safavids preserved their empire and left a legacy of resilience in the face of adversity.

Chapter 13: Tsarist Secret Police

By the late 19th century, Tsarist Russia was a sprawling empire, a patchwork of ethnicities and cultures that stretched from Eastern Europe to the Pacific Ocean. Yet, beneath the grandeur of the Tsar's court and the vast expanse of his territories lay deep unrest. Industrialization was creating a new working class that lived in squalor, while the rigid autocracy stifled calls for reform. Revolutionary ideologies like socialism and anarchism found fertile ground among the oppressed. Adding to the turmoil, foreign powers sought to destabilize Russia, covertly supporting revolutionary factions in hopes of weakening the empire. To counter these growing threats, the Tsar relied on the Okhrana, his secret police, to uncover and dismantle the networks plotting the empire's downfall.

The Okhrana, officially known as the Department for Protecting Public Security and Order, operated both within Russia and abroad. Its agents infiltrated revolutionary groups, monitored dissidents, and intercepted foreign aid meant for subversive movements. While brutal in its methods, the Okhrana's mission was to prevent the empire's collapse by any means necessary. Among its ranks was a man known only by the codename "Orlov," an experienced operative who would become a key figure in foiling one of the most dangerous threats to Tsarist Russia.

By the early 1900s, revolutionary fervor was reaching a fever pitch. Groups like the Socialist Revolutionaries (SRs) and anarchist cells carried out assassinations and bombings, targeting government officials and industrialists. Reports from Paris, a hub for Russian exiles and revolutionaries, indicated that foreign powers were quietly funneling money and resources to these groups. The Okhrana tasked Orlov, a master of disguise and fluent in multiple languages, with infiltrating the émigré networks in Paris to uncover their backers and thwart their plans.

Disguised as a disillusioned nobleman, Orlov made his way to Paris, blending into the city's vibrant Russian émigré community. Paris was a hotbed of revolutionary activity, with intellectuals, activists, and exiles gathering in cafes and salons to debate the future of Russia. Orlov began frequenting these gatherings, earning the trust of key figures within the Socialist Revolutionaries. His cover story—a former aristocrat turned sympathizer—allowed him to move freely among the revolutionaries without raising suspicion.

Through careful observation and subtle questioning, Orlov uncovered a web of connections linking the SRs to foreign financiers. A French industrialist with ties to the government was funding the publication of revolutionary newspapers and pamphlets, which were smuggled into Russia to stir unrest among workers and peasants. Additionally, a British arms dealer was supplying weapons to revolutionary cells in Moscow and St. Petersburg. These revelations confirmed the Okhrana's suspicions that foreign interests were fueling the revolutionary fire.

Orlov reported his findings to his superiors in St. Petersburg through coded messages. Armed with this intelligence, the Okhrana launched a coordinated operation to dismantle the revolutionary networks. In Russia, key operatives were arrested, and caches of smuggled weapons were seized. In Paris, the Russian embassy pressured the French government to investigate the industrialist supporting the revolutionaries. Although reluctant at first, French authorities eventually intervened, forcing the industrialist to withdraw his support and disrupting the flow of funds to the SRs.

While Orlov's work disrupted revolutionary activities in Paris, a more immediate threat was brewing in London. A group of anarchists, supported by a wealthy British benefactor, was planning an assassination attempt on a high-ranking Russian official during his visit to Paris. The plot involved a coordinated bombing and the use of firearms, with the goal of not only killing the official but also igniting a wave of revolutionary violence across Europe.

The Okhrana dispatched Orlov to London, where he infiltrated the anarchist group by posing as a courier for their communications. Over several weeks, he gained the trust of the group's leaders and learned the details of their plan. The assassination was scheduled to take place at a public reception in Paris, with explosives hidden in a carriage that would detonate as the official arrived.

Orlov acted swiftly. He intercepted key communications and passed the information to the Russian embassy in Paris. French police, working closely with the Okhrana, arrested the anarchists involved in the plot and confiscated their explosives. The British benefactor, once exposed, faced public scandal and withdrew his support for revolutionary activities. The assassination attempt was foiled, and the coordinated response demonstrated the Okhrana's reach and effectiveness.

Despite these successes, Orlov's work revealed the limitations of the Okhrana's approach. The secret police relied heavily on infiltration and surveillance, but their methods often involved brutal crackdowns and the use of double agents who incited violence to justify government action. These tactics, while effective in the short term, deepened public resentment toward the Tsarist regime. Many ordinary Russians viewed the Okhrana as an oppressive force, fueling the very revolutionary fervor it sought to extinguish.

By 1905, the tensions that Orlov and his colleagues had worked to contain erupted into revolution. Strikes, protests, and uprisings swept across the empire, forcing Tsar Nicholas II to grant limited reforms, including the establishment of a parliamentary body, the Duma. Although the revolution subsided, it left deep scars, and the underlying causes of unrest remained unresolved. Orlov's work had delayed the collapse of the regime, but the cracks in the foundation of Tsarist Russia were becoming impossible to ignore.

Orlov's career with the Okhrana ended as the empire's challenges grew insurmountable. The revolutionary movements he had fought against continued to evolve, gaining strength and support both domestically and internationally. By 1917, the Russian Empire would collapse under the weight of revolution, war, and internal decay. Orlov's efforts to preserve the Tsarist regime, though heroic in their own way, were ultimately unable to prevent the inevitable.

The story of Orlov and the Okhrana is a testament to the complexities of espionage in a time of upheaval. While the secret police succeeded in foiling plots and disrupting revolutionary networks, their methods also contributed to the atmosphere of fear and oppression that fueled dissent. Orlov's work, carried out in the shadows, delayed the fall of the empire and showcased the power of intelligence in shaping history. Yet, it also highlights the limits of statecraft when faced with deep-seated social and political discontent.

In the end, the Okhrana's mission was a paradox: to maintain order in a system that was inherently unsustainable. Orlov's story stands as a reminder that while espionage can shape events and buy time, it cannot solve the fundamental problems that drive revolution and change.

Chapter 14: Civil Action

The American Civil War, raging from 1861 to 1865, was not only a battle between the Union and the Confederacy but also a precarious diplomatic game played on the international stage. For the Union, maintaining foreign neutrality was essential. A European alliance with the Confederacy could spell disaster, providing the Southern states with the resources, recognition, and legitimacy they desperately sought. Among the nations being courted by Confederate envoys, Britain and France stood out as the most significant. Both countries had strong economic ties to the South due to its cotton exports, and both saw opportunities to weaken the United States by encouraging its division.

In this volatile environment, the Union needed skilled diplomats to ensure that no European power sided with the Confederacy. Charles Francis Adams, the United States ambassador to Britain, was one of the key figures in this effort. Adams, a member of the illustrious Adams family and the son of former President John Quincy Adams, carried the weight of his legacy into his role. Over the course of the war, his diplomatic efforts would Play a pivotal role in preventing British recognition of the Confederacy and averting a potential global conflict.

When Adams arrived in London in 1861, the situation was dire. Confederate envoys, including James Mason and John Slidell, had already begun lobbying British officials, arguing that the South's cotton exports were essential to Britain's textile industry. They emphasized that Britain's neutrality—or worse, its support for the Union blockade of Southern ports—would lead to economic disaster for British workers and manufacturers. At the same time, they sought to portray the Confederacy as a legitimate nation fighting for self-determination, a cause they hoped would resonate with Britain's values.

Adams understood the stakes. If Britain recognized the Confederacy, it could open the door for other European powers, particularly France, to follow suit. Such recognition would provide the South with crucial diplomatic support and potentially lead to military or economic aid. Worse, it could embolden Britain to challenge the Union's naval blockade, leading to direct confrontation and possibly dragging Europe into the conflict.

Adams began his mission by establishing himself as a steady and reliable presence in London. He approached his role with a calm professionalism, avoiding heated rhetoric while quietly building relationships with key British officials. Among these officials was Lord John Russell, Britain's Foreign Secretary, whose influence would be crucial in shaping the government's stance on the Civil War. Russell was sympathetic to the Confederacy's arguments but cautious about taking any action that might lead to war with the Union.

The first major test of Adams' diplomacy came with the Trent Affair in late 1861. A Union naval officer, Captain Charles Wilkes, intercepted the British mail packet Trent and forcibly removed Mason and Slidell, who were on their way to Europe to represent the Confederacy. The incident sparked outrage in Britain, with many viewing it as a blatant violation of neutral rights. British newspapers demanded retaliation, and war seemed a real possibility.

Adams worked tirelessly to defuse the crisis. He reminded British officials that the Union's actions, though controversial,

were not intended as an affront to Britain. At the same time,
he quietly urged Washington to release the Confederate
envoys as a gesture of goodwill. President Lincoln,
recognizing the gravity of the situation, agreed to free Mason
and Slidell, averting a diplomatic rupture. The resolution of the
Trent Affair demonstrated Adams' ability to navigate delicate
situations and maintain peace between the Union and Britain.

While Adams focused on diplomacy, the Union also relied on
intelligence and covert operations to counter Confederate
efforts in Europe. Union operatives monitored Confederate
agents and intercepted their communications, providing
Adams with valuable insights into their strategies. For
example, Union intelligence uncovered that the Confederacy
was attempting to purchase warships from British shipbuilders,
including the infamous Alabama, a commerce raider designed
to attack Union merchant ships.

Armed with this information, Adams launched a determined
campaign to prevent the sale of these ships. He presented
evidence to the British government, arguing that allowing the

construction of Confederate warships violated Britain's neutrality. In one memorable exchange, Adams confronted Lord Russell with proof of the Alabama's purpose, warning that its launch would constitute an unfriendly act. His persistence paid off; while the Alabama eventually escaped to sea, other Confederate ships under construction were seized by British authorities before they could be delivered.

France presented another challenge. Emperor Napoleon III, seeking to expand his influence in the Americas, was sympathetic to the Confederacy. The French emperor entertained the idea of recognizing the Southern states, particularly if Britain did so first. Confederate agents worked hard to convince Napoleon that a divided United States would be less able to interfere in European affairs, particularly in Mexico, where France was establishing a puppet regime under Emperor Maximilian I.

To counter this, Adams coordinated with William L. Dayton, the U.S. ambassador to France. Together, they emphasized the Union's commitment to preserving the Monroe Doctrine, which opposed European interference in the Americas. They also warned that any recognition of the Confederacy would likely lead to conflict with the Union, jeopardizing France's interests in the region. These efforts, combined with the lack of British recognition, persuaded Napoleon to adopt a cautious approach, avoiding open support for the Confederacy.

As the war progressed, Adams and his counterparts leveraged Union military victories to strengthen their diplomatic position. The Battle of Antietam in September 1862 and President Lincoln's subsequent issuance of the Emancipation Proclamation were turning points. The proclamation reframed the war as a fight against slavery, making it politically difficult for Britain or France to support the Confederacy, which was now clearly aligned with the institution of slavery. Adams capitalized on this shift, using it to rally British abolitionist groups and sway public opinion against the South.

By 1863, the Confederacy's hopes for European recognition had faded. Adams' steady diplomacy, combined with Union military successes and strategic use of intelligence, had effectively neutralized the Confederate threat in Europe. Britain and France remained neutral, and the Union blockade of Southern ports tightened, further weakening the Confederacy's economy and war effort.

Adams' work in London was not without challenges. He faced constant pressure from Confederate agents, as well as skepticism from British officials who doubted the Union's ability to win the war. Yet his persistence, integrity, and ability to navigate complex political dynamics ensured that the Union's message was heard. He maintained a delicate balance, advocating firmly for the Union's interests while avoiding the kind of antagonism that could have pushed Britain into the Confederate camp.

When the Civil War ended in 1865, Adams returned to the United States, his mission accomplished. His efforts had prevented foreign intervention, ensuring that the conflict remained a domestic affair. By keeping Britain and France on the sidelines, Adams and his fellow diplomats had averted a potential global conflict, allowing the Union to focus its

resources on defeating the Confederacy.

Chapter 15: The Great Game

In the 19th century, Central Asia became the stage for one of

the most high-stakes geopolitical rivalries of the age, known

as the Great Game. This clandestine struggle pitted the British

Empire against Imperial Russia, as both sought to expand

their influence into the buffer zones of Afghanistan and the

surrounding regions. For Britain, Afghanistan was the

keystone of India's security, the crown jewel of its empire. For

Russia, it was a strategic frontier, a gateway to potentially

disrupting Britain's dominance in South Asia. While both

empires avoided full-scale war, their contest played out in the

shadows, where spies, envoys, and adventurers worked to

outmaneuver each other in the mountainous terrain of

Afghanistan.

Among the operatives dispatched by Britain was Alexander Burnes, a young Scottish officer with a knack for languages and a reputation for charm. Known as "Bokhara Burnes" after his travels in Central Asia, he was one of the most celebrated agents of the Great Game. Burnes was tasked with one of the most delicate missions of the era: to maintain Afghanistan as a neutral buffer state, preventing it from falling into Russian hands without provoking a direct confrontation.

Burnes arrived in Kabul in the early 1830s, ostensibly as a merchant seeking to establish trade routes. His true purpose, however, was far more complex. The British government feared that Dost Mohammad Khan, the ruler of Afghanistan, might align with Russia to counterbalance the growing threat from British-controlled India. Russian envoys had already begun courting the Afghan leader, offering military and economic assistance in exchange for an alliance. Burnes' mission was to undermine these efforts, using diplomacy and subterfuge to keep Afghanistan from tipping into Russia's sphere of influence.

Burnes' first task was to win the trust of Dost Mohammad. Fluent in Persian and Pashto, Burnes used his linguistic skills and cultural sensitivity to ingratiate himself with the Afghan court. He presented Britain as a benevolent partner, capable of providing trade opportunities and protection against regional rivals. However, Burnes quickly discovered that Dost Mohammad was deeply concerned about the loss of Peshawar, a key Afghan territory that had been seized by the Sikh Empire. The Afghan leader sought British support in reclaiming the city, a demand that placed Burnes in a precarious position. Supporting Afghanistan against the Sikhs risked antagonizing a British ally, while refusing could push Dost Mohammad closer to Russia.

To complicate matters, a Russian envoy, Ivan Vitkevich, arrived in Kabul shortly after Burnes. Vitkevich, a seasoned diplomat, brought promises of arms and alliances, positioning Russia as a more reliable partner than Britain. The Afghan court buzzed with intrigue as Burnes and Vitkevich vied for influence, each attempting to outmaneuver the other without revealing the full extent of their motives. It was a dance of nations, played out in whispered conversations and secret agreements.

Burnes relied on his network of local informants to monitor Vitkevich's activities and counter Russian overtures. He spread rumors among the Afghan elite, suggesting that Russia's promises were hollow and that its true aim was to dominate Afghanistan as a vassal state. At the same time, Burnes worked to stall Dost Mohammad's negotiations with Vitkevich, urging the British government to offer concessions that might sway the Afghan leader. However, London was slow to act, unwilling to commit to military support or risk escalating tensions with Russia.

As the months dragged on, Burnes found himself increasingly isolated. His position in Kabul became untenable when Dost Mohammad, frustrated by Britain's lack of support, formally opened negotiations with Vitkevich. Burnes was recalled to India, his mission deemed a failure. However, his efforts had not been entirely in vain. The intelligence he gathered during his time in Kabul provided valuable insights into Afghan politics and Russian strategies, shaping British policy in the years to come.

The rivalry between Britain and Russia continued to escalate, culminating in the First Anglo-Afghan War (1839–1842). Burnes returned to Kabul as part of the British-backed effort to install a puppet ruler, Shah Shuja, on the Afghan throne. While initially successful, the occupation quickly turned into a disaster, as Afghan resistance grew and the British found themselves cut off in hostile territory. Burnes, who had tried to warn his superiors about the fragility of their position, became a scapegoat for the campaign's failures. He was assassinated in 1841 during a revolt in Kabul, his death a grim reminder of the dangers faced by those who operated in the shadows of the Great Game.

Despite the tragic end to Burnes' career, his legacy as a key figure in the Great Game endures. His work in Afghanistan exemplified the delicate balance required to navigate a world where diplomacy, espionage, and military power intersected. Burnes' ability to adapt to shifting circumstances, build relationships, and gather intelligence made him one of the most effective agents of his time, even if his successes were often overshadowed by the failures of British policy.

The Great Game continued for decades, with British and Russian agents vying for influence in Central Asia through a combination of diplomacy, espionage, and covert action. While the contest never escalated into a full-scale war, it shaped the geopolitics of the region and left a lasting legacy of mistrust and instability. Afghanistan, caught between two empires, became a symbol of the perils of imperial ambition and the resilience of those who sought to maintain their independence.

Chapter 16: The Peace of Kings

By the late 19th century, the Austro-Hungarian Empire was a precarious colossus, held together by the delicate thread of Habsburg rule. Its vast territory encompassed dozens of ethnic groups—Germans, Hungarians, Czechs, Slovaks, Poles, Serbs, Croats, and more—each with their own languages, traditions, and grievances. Nationalist movements, inspired by the liberal revolutions of Europe, simmered across the empire, threatening to pull it apart. The monarchy, desperate to maintain its grip on power, turned to a potent combination of intelligence, espionage, and diplomacy to hold its diverse subjects together.

At the center of this effort was the Evidenzbureau, the Austro-Hungarian Empire's military intelligence agency. Founded in 1850, the agency had a clear mandate: to identify and disrupt threats to the state, both internal and external. Its officers infiltrated nationalist movements, intercepted communications, and worked behind the scenes to manipulate political and social dynamics. While heavy-handed repression often characterized the empire's response to dissent, the Evidenzbureau operated in the shadows, using subtlety and strategy to prevent uprisings before they could erupt.

The Balkans were a particular flashpoint. The annexation of Bosnia and Herzegovina in 1908 had intensified tensions with Serbian nationalists, who dreamed of uniting South Slavic peoples under their leadership. These ambitions were backed by Russia, which positioned itself as the protector of Slavs and sought to weaken Austria-Hungary in the region. Serbian agents smuggled weapons and propaganda into Bosnia, stoking unrest among the local population. To counter this, the Evidenzbureau dispatched its best operatives, including an agent known by the codename "Klaus," to monitor and disrupt nationalist activity.

Klaus, a veteran intelligence officer, was fluent in Serbo-Croatian and deeply familiar with Balkan politics. Disguised as a merchant, he infiltrated the networks of Serbian agitators operating in Bosnia. Over months of careful observation and subtle questioning, he uncovered a smuggling operation supplying arms to radical groups planning attacks on Austro-Hungarian officials. Klaus also discovered that these efforts were funded in part by Russian operatives, who were using the unrest as a proxy to undermine the Habsburg monarchy.

Klaus relayed his findings to Vienna through coded messages, enabling the Evidenzbureau to coordinate a series of raids that dismantled the smuggling network and arrested key agitators. However, Klaus cautioned against relying solely on repression. He recognized that heavy-handed crackdowns risked alienating moderate factions within the nationalist movement and driving more people into the arms of the radicals. Instead, he advocated for a dual approach: using intelligence to isolate extremists while engaging moderates through negotiation and reform.

This strategy was put to the test in 1910, when Klaus uncovered a plot to assassinate an Austro-Hungarian governor during a public event in Sarajevo. The conspirators, a mix of local radicals and Serbian operatives, aimed to ignite a broader rebellion against Habsburg rule. Klaus infiltrated the group and gained the trust of its leaders, learning the details of their plan. Rather than immediately arrest the plotters, he worked with local authorities to stage a sting operation, intercepting the attackers just before they could act. The plot was foiled, but the arrests were handled quietly to avoid inflaming public sentiment.

The Habsburg monarchy, recognizing the value of Klaus's intelligence, used his insights to open back-channel negotiations with moderate nationalist leaders. These figures, while advocating for greater autonomy, were opposed to the violence promoted by radical factions. Through intermediaries, Austrian officials offered concessions such as increased local governance and cultural protections for Slavic communities. While these negotiations were fraught with tension, they succeeded in defusing some of the immediate unrest and weakening the radicals' appeal.

The Evidenzbureau also targeted the flow of foreign propaganda into the empire. Russian agents were spreading pamphlets and newspapers emphasizing Slavic solidarity and calling for rebellion against Austrian rule. To counter this, Klaus and his colleagues launched a disinformation campaign, highlighting the hardships faced by Slavs under Russian rule and portraying Austria-Hungary as a more stable and benevolent protector of their interests. These efforts, combined with increased surveillance of printing presses and border checkpoints, helped to stem the tide of subversive material.

Despite these successes, the challenges facing the Evidenzbureau were immense. The empire's sheer diversity made surveillance and infiltration a daunting task. Agents often struggled with linguistic and cultural barriers, and nationalist movements adapted quickly to avoid detection. The rise of modern technology, particularly the telegraph and mass printing, allowed dissent to spread more rapidly than ever before. Klaus and his colleagues worked tirelessly to keep pace, intercepting communications and planting counter-narratives wherever possible.

In addition to external threats, the empire faced internal divisions between its two dominant groups: the Austrians and the Hungarians. The 1867 Ausgleich (Compromise) that created the dual monarchy had granted significant autonomy to Hungary, but this arrangement left other ethnic groups feeling marginalized. The Evidenzbureau monitored these tensions closely, providing intelligence that helped the government implement policies aimed at placating minority groups. These included investments in infrastructure and education in Slavic regions, as well as symbolic gestures like appointing Slavic officials to prominent positions.

Klaus's work came to a tragic end with the assassination of Archduke Franz Ferdinand in Sarajevo in 1914, an event that would plunge Europe into the First World War. The assassination, carried out by members of the Black Hand, a Serbian nationalist organization, highlighted the limits of espionage and diplomacy in the face of radicalism and escalating tensions. Klaus, who had long warned of the growing threat posed by Serbian nationalists, saw his efforts overshadowed by the march of history.

The assassination set off a chain reaction that the Habsburg monarchy could not control. Austria-Hungary's harsh response to Serbia, backed by Germany, led to a confrontation with Russia and its allies, dragging the continent into a catastrophic war. The empire that Klaus had fought to preserve would not survive the conflict, its dissolution driven by the same nationalist forces he had worked so hard to contain.

The legacy of Klaus and the Evidenzbureau lies in their ability to navigate the complexities of a multiethnic empire during an era of rising nationalism. Through intelligence and negotiation, they delayed the fragmentation of Austria-Hungary, preserving its unity for decades longer than many had thought possible. Their work highlights the power of espionage not only to prevent violence but also to foster dialogue and compromise in the face of seemingly insurmountable challenges.

Yet, the story of Austria-Hungary is also a cautionary tale. The empire's reliance on repression and manipulation, while effective in the short term, ultimately failed to address the deeper grievances of its subjects. The nationalism that Klaus sought to contain could not be extinguished by force or subterfuge; it was a tide that would sweep away the old order and reshape the map of Europe.

World War I was a cataclysm that shook Europe to its core. The horrors of trench warfare, the unrelenting carnage, and the monumental strains on economies and societies brought the great powers to the brink of collapse. Germany, at the heart of the conflict, faced not only external pressures from the Allied forces but also growing unrest within its borders. The war drained its resources, crippled its economy, and left its population teetering on the edge of rebellion. As mutinies simmered among soldiers and workers' strikes spread through cities, the German Empire turned to its shadowy agents—the intelligence operatives working in silence to hold the nation together.

Germany's intelligence services, including the Abteilung IIIb (the military intelligence branch) and the Polizeidirektion Berlin, played a critical role in navigating the storm. While much of their work focused on gathering information about enemy movements, a significant portion was dedicated to countering internal threats that could destabilize the empire. In this war of endurance, these quiet men worked to manipulate public opinion, disrupt revolutionary movements, and prevent Germany from descending into chaos.

By 1917, the strain on Germany was evident. The British naval blockade had choked off vital supplies, leading to severe food shortages. Hunger riots broke out in major cities, and resentment against the ruling elite grew. The Social Democratic Party (SPD) and other socialist factions gained traction, calling for an end to the war. Even within the military, discontent brewed as soldiers grew weary of the endless slaughter. The specter of revolution loomed, threatening to dismantle the empire from within.

The Intelligence services understood that maintaining order required more than brute force. Repression alone risked driving dissent underground, where it would be harder to control. Instead, they adopted a strategy of infiltration and manipulation, using covert means to weaken revolutionary movements and redirect public anger away from the state.

One of the most pressing challenges came from the Independent Social Democratic Party of Germany (USPD), a radical offshoot of the SPD that openly opposed the war. The USPD had ties to labor unions and was instrumental in organizing strikes that disrupted war production. German operatives, posing as sympathetic workers, infiltrated the party's ranks to gather intelligence about its plans and leadership. By identifying key agitators, the government was able to preempt major strikes through targeted arrests and the co-opting of union leaders.

In Berlin, the Polizeidirektion, led by experienced officers skilled in counterintelligence, monitored socialist meeting halls and printing presses. They intercepted pamphlets calling for mass protests and disseminated their own counter-narratives, portraying the USPD as traitors working to undermine Germany's war effort. These efforts, while not entirely successful, slowed the momentum of the socialist movement and kept critical industries running.

Another significant threat came from soldiers returning from the front. Disillusioned and embittered, many of these men became fertile ground for revolutionary ideologies. German intelligence operatives embedded within military units worked to identify ringleaders of mutinies and used a combination of persuasion and coercion to maintain discipline. In one notable case, agents discovered plans for a coordinated mutiny in a major garrison near Cologne. By leaking misinformation suggesting that the ringleaders were under surveillance, the operatives sowed fear among the conspirators, causing the plot to unravel before it could be executed.

While domestic unrest consumed much of their attention, German intelligence also faced the challenge of managing ethnic minorities within the empire. Poles, Alsatians, and other groups chafed under German rule, viewing the war as an opportunity to push for greater autonomy or even independence. To counter these movements, operatives used a mix of surveillance and propaganda to sow divisions within minority communities. They highlighted the risks of rebellion, suggesting that a postwar Germany would be more likely to grant concessions to loyal subjects than to those who betrayed the empire.

Despite their efforts, the tide of discontent continued to rise. In early 1918, a wave of strikes swept through Berlin and other industrial centers, paralyzing the war economy. The intelligence services responded by working closely with industrialists and conservative labor leaders to negotiate temporary compromises, such as higher wages and improved working conditions. At the same time, they intensified their propaganda efforts, using newspapers and posters to frame the strikes as unpatriotic acts that endangered soldiers on the front lines. This dual approach managed to defuse the immediate crisis, but it was clear that Germany was approaching its breaking point.

The most critical test came in November 1918, as the war drew to a close. Germany's defeat was imminent, and the empire teetered on the brink of revolution. The abdication of Kaiser Wilhelm II created a power vacuum that radical factions sought to exploit. Workers' councils, inspired by the Russian

Soviets, sprang up across the country, calling for a socialist state. The intelligence services, now operating in a state of near-panic, launched a final effort to prevent total collapse.

Agents infiltrated the workers' councils to gather intelligence and sow discord among their leaders. They spread rumors that the councils were being manipulated by foreign powers, particularly Bolshevik Russia, to undermine Germany. At the same time, they worked to bolster moderate factions within the SPD, who advocated for a democratic republic rather than a socialist revolution. This covert support helped the SPD consolidate power, enabling it to negotiate a transition that avoided the kind of violent upheaval seen in Russia.

One of the most effective tools in the intelligence arsenal was disinformation. German operatives planted stories in the press suggesting that revolutionary leaders were embezzling funds or colluding with foreign agents. These allegations, while often fabricated, undermined public trust in the revolutionaries and weakened their support base. The intelligence services also used their networks to redirect public anger toward scapegoats, such as war profiteers and the Allies, diverting attention away from the government's failures.

In the end, Germany avoided the kind of total collapse that many had feared. The establishment of the Weimar Republic brought an uneasy stability, though it came at the cost of the empire's dissolution and significant territorial losses. The intelligence services, despite their efforts, could not prevent the ultimate downfall of the German monarchy. However, their actions during the final years of the war bought crucial time, preventing a descent into chaos that might have spread across Europe.

The legacy of Germany's intelligence operatives during World War I is a complex one. On one hand, their efforts to maintain order and disrupt revolutionary movements helped to avert an immediate crisis. On the other hand, their reliance on manipulation and repression deepened societal divisions and sowed the seeds of future unrest. The disinformation campaigns and surveillance tactics they employed would later be adopted by more authoritarian regimes, including the Nazis, who used them to devastating effect.

The story of the "quiet men" who worked in the shadows highlights the power and limitations of espionage in times of crisis. Intelligence can shape events and influence outcomes, but it cannot address the underlying causes of discontent. In the case of Germany, the pressures of war, economic collapse, and social inequality proved too great for any intelligence service to contain.

As World War I came to an end, the quiet men faded into the background, their work overshadowed by the tumultuous events that followed. Yet, their legacy endures as a testament to the complex interplay between war, politics, and intelligence—a reminder that even in the darkest times, the shadows can hold the fate of nations.

Chapter 18: Allied Agents

World War II was a conflict defined not only by its battles but also by the unseen war waged in the shadows. Intelligence played a decisive role in shaping the outcome, and nowhere was this more evident than in the lead-up to D-Day, the Allied invasion of Normandy in June 1944. As the largest amphibious assault in history, the success of Operation Overlord depended not only on military might but also on the ability to deceive the Nazis about the true location and timing of the landings. At the heart of this deception was a network of MI5 operatives and double agents who created a tapestry of lies so convincing that it diverted German forces and ensured the Allies a critical foothold in Europe.

By 1943, the Allies were preparing to retake Western Europe from Nazi control. The beaches of Normandy had been chosen as the invasion site, but this decision carried immense risk. German defenses along the Atlantic Wall were formidable, and an accurate German response could spell disaster for the operation. To mitigate this, the Allies launched Operation Bodyguard, a comprehensive deception strategy designed to mislead the Germans about their intentions. One of its key components, Operation Fortitude, focused on convincing the Nazis that the invasion would occur in the Pas de Calais, far from Normandy.

The success of this plan hinged on the work of double agents—spies who had ostensibly defected to the Nazis but were, in reality, working for MI5. These agents formed the backbone of the British Double-Cross System, a program that turned captured or recruited enemy spies into tools of Allied deception. Among these operatives, a few stood out for their pivotal roles in the success of D-Day.

One of the most influential double agents was Juan Pujol García, codenamed "Garbo" by the British and "Alaric" by the Germans. A Spaniard with a flair for storytelling, Garbo had managed to convince the Germans that he was a dedicated Nazi sympathizer. Over time, he built an extensive network of fictitious sub-agents, all feeding fabricated intelligence to the Abwehr, Germany's military intelligence service. In reality, Garbo was working for MI5, and his fictional network was entirely a product of his imagination, crafted with meticulous detail to give it credibility.

As D-Day approached, Garbo's reports became critical to the success of Operation Fortitude. Through carefully planted messages, he convinced the Germans that the Allies were massing troops in southeastern England, preparing to invade the Pas de Calais. To reinforce this deception, Garbo provided details about fake military units, including the entirely fictitious First U.S. Army Group (FUSAG), supposedly commanded by General George S. Patton. The Germans, already wary of Patton's reputation as a bold and aggressive leader, readily believed that he would lead the main assault.

Another key player in the deception was Roman Czerniawski, codenamed "Brutus," a Polish officer who had initially worked as a spy for the French Resistance before being captured by the Nazis. After convincing the Germans to let him operate as a double agent, Czerniawski was turned by MI5. Like Garbo, Brutus fed the Germans a steady stream of false information, reinforcing the illusion of an invasion at the Pas de Calais. His reports, combined with those of other double agents, helped to create a cohesive narrative that kept German forces focused on the wrong location.

The deception went beyond mere reports. Operation Fortitude relied on a combination of fake radio transmissions, dummy equipment, and visual tricks to sell the illusion. Inflatable tanks and trucks were placed in fields across southeastern England, while fake landing craft were positioned in ports along the coastline. The Allies even went so far as to construct dummy airfields, complete with wooden planes, to suggest that an invasion force was preparing to launch from the area.

Meanwhile, MI5 worked tirelessly to ensure that the Germans trusted their double agents. The Double-Cross System had cultivated a reputation for reliability by occasionally allowing small, inconsequential pieces of genuine intelligence to reach the Germans, giving their operatives credibility. By 1944, the Abwehr considered agents like Garbo and Brutus to be among their most reliable sources, a testament to the skill with which MI5 managed these operations.

As the date for D-Day drew closer, the Allies intensified their efforts to mislead the Germans. In late May and early June 1944, Garbo sent a series of urgent messages to his handlers, warning them that the invasion was imminent but would occur in the Pas de Calais. These reports were timed to coincide with other elements of the deception plan, including increased fake radio traffic and the movement of dummy equipment. The Germans, convinced by the consistency of the information, redeployed significant forces to the Pas de Calais, leaving Normandy less heavily defended.

The success of Operation Fortitude became evident on June 6, 1944, when the Allies launched their assault on Normandy. While the landings were met with fierce resistance, the German response was disjointed and delayed. Crucially, Adolf Hitler, still convinced that the main invasion would occur at the Pas de Calais, refused to release additional reinforcements to Normandy. Even after the landings were underway, German forces in the Pas de Calais remained on high alert, waiting for an invasion that would never come.

The role of the double agents did not end with D-Day. In the weeks that followed, they continued to feed the Germans false information, suggesting that the Normandy landings were merely a diversion and that the real assault was still to come. This prolonged the Germans' hesitation, allowing the Allies to establish a secure beachhead and push further into occupied France. By the time the Germans realized they had been deceived, it was too late to recover.

The Impact of the Double-Cross System and the work of operatives like Garbo and Brutus cannot be overstated. Their efforts were instrumental in ensuring the success of Operation Overlord, which marked the beginning of the end for Nazi Germany. By diverting German forces and delaying their response, these agents saved countless Allied lives and accelerated the liberation of Europe.

Yet, the work of these operatives came at a personal cost. The stress of living double lives, constantly under the threat of exposure, took its toll. Garbo, who had become a hero to the Allies, struggled with the psychological burden of his role after the war. He faked his death in the 1950s and lived in obscurity for decades before being rediscovered in the 1980s. Brutus, too, faced challenges reintegrating into civilian life, his contributions overshadowed by the broader narrative of the war.

The story of the double agents of D-Day is a testament to the power of intelligence and deception in warfare. Their ability to manipulate perceptions and shape enemy decisions highlights the critical role of espionage in achieving strategic objectives. While their work was hidden from view, its impact was felt on the beaches of Normandy and across the battlefields of Europe.

As World War II drew to a close, the efforts of these operatives became part of the larger legacy of the Allied victory. They remind us that wars are not won solely through battles and bravery, but also through the quiet, meticulous work of those who operate in the shadows. The double agents of D-Day were the architects of a deception that altered the course of history, securing the path to peace through the art of espionage.

Chapter 19: Covert Action in Cuba

The Cuban Missile Crisis of October 1962 was the closest the world ever came to nuclear annihilation. For thirteen tense days, the United States and the Soviet Union stood on the brink of war, locked in a high-stakes standoff over Soviet missile installations in Cuba. While the leaders of both superpowers, John F. Kennedy and Nikita Khrushchev, exchanged ultimatums, a hidden network of spies, diplomats, and back-channel negotiators worked tirelessly behind the scenes to avert disaster. Their actions, carried out in secrecy and often without fanfare, secured a fragile peace and saved the world from catastrophe.

The crisis began when American U-2 reconnaissance planes captured images of Soviet missile sites under construction in

Cuba. These medium- and intermediate-range ballistic missiles had the potential to deliver nuclear warheads to most of the continental United States within minutes. President Kennedy and his advisors immediately recognized the existential threat posed by these installations. A naval blockade, euphemistically called a "quarantine," was imposed to prevent further shipments of weapons to Cuba, while the U.S. demanded the immediate removal of the missiles already there.

As tensions mounted, the intelligence communities of both nations became crucial players in the unfolding drama. In Washington, the CIA scrambled to gather more intelligence about the missile sites and Soviet activities in Cuba. Covert operatives on the ground provided critical information about the pace of construction and the operational status of the missiles. Their reports revealed that some missiles were already operational, intensifying the urgency of the situation.

One of the unsung heroes of the crisis was Oleg Penkovsky, a Soviet military intelligence officer secretly working for Western intelligence agencies. Months before the crisis, Penkovsky had provided the CIA and MI6 with detailed information about Soviet missile capabilities, including the specifications and deployment patterns of the missiles now in Cuba. This intelligence allowed the U.S. to assess the threat accurately and develop countermeasures. Penkovsky's betrayal came at a high cost; he was arrested by the KGB during the crisis and executed the following year. Yet, his contributions were instrumental in shaping the U.S. response.

Meanwhile, in Moscow, the KGB monitored American military movements and political decisions, seeking to gauge how far Kennedy was willing to go to force the removal of the missiles. Soviet operatives also worked covertly in Cuba, ensuring the secrecy of the missile installations and preparing for possible American sabotage. Their efforts were matched by the CIA, which infiltrated exile groups in Florida to assess the feasibility of a ground invasion or covert action to disable the missile sites.

As military forces on both sides were placed on high alert, the possibility of a catastrophic miscalculation loomed. The most dangerous moment came on October 27, 1962, a day later called "Black Saturday." On that day, a U-2 reconnaissance plane strayed into Soviet airspace, triggering a scramble of Soviet fighter jets. At the same time, another U-2 was shot down over Cuba, killing its pilot, Major Rudolf Anderson Jr. The downing of the plane could have been a pretext for war, but Kennedy chose to respond with restraint, recognizing the need to de-escalate the situation.

Behind the scenes, covert back-channel negotiations were already underway. One of the most critical exchanges occurred between KGB officer Aleksandr Fomin (an alias for Alexander Feklisov) and ABC journalist John Scali in Washington. Using Scali as an intermediary, Fomin floated a proposal: the Soviets would remove the missiles from Cuba in exchange for a U.S. pledge not to invade the island. This unofficial channel allowed both sides to explore solutions without the pressure of public scrutiny or political posturing.

Simultaneously, American diplomat Llewellyn Thompson played a pivotal role in shaping Kennedy's approach. Thompson, a former ambassador to the Soviet Union, had a deep understanding of Khrushchev's psychology and motives. He urged Kennedy to focus on Khrushchev's desire to avoid humiliation and suggested offering a secret concession to sweeten the deal. This advice led to the inclusion of a quiet agreement to remove U.S. Jupiter missiles from Turkey as part of the resolution, though this concession would remain secret to protect NATO unity.

In Cuba, covert operatives continued to work under immense pressure. A network of Cuban exiles, supported by the CIA, relayed intelligence about the missile sites' progress and the movements of Soviet personnel. Their information helped U.S. analysts verify Soviet claims during the negotiations, ensuring that the Americans were not deceived. At the same time, Soviet technicians worked day and night to complete the missile installations, aware that the longer the crisis dragged on, the greater the risk of an American strike.

The resolution of the crisis came on October 28, 1962, when Khrushchev announced that the Soviet Union would dismantle the missile sites in Cuba in exchange for a U.S. guarantee not to invade the island. The secret agreement to remove the Jupiter missiles from Turkey was not disclosed at the time, allowing both leaders to claim victory. The covert efforts of diplomats, spies, and intermediaries had succeeded in steering the world away from the brink.

While Kennedy and Khrushchev received much of the credit for resolving the crisis, the contributions of intelligence operatives and back-channel negotiators were equally critical. Their ability to navigate the shadows, gather vital information, and communicate discreetly ensured that both sides had the clarity needed to avoid miscalculation. In a conflict defined by brinkmanship, it was the quiet work of these individuals that preserved peace.

The legacy of the Cuban Missile Crisis lies not only in its resolution but also in the lessons it imparted about the importance of communication, restraint, and intelligence in averting catastrophe. The crisis prompted the establishment of the Moscow-Washington hotline, a direct communication link between the superpowers, to reduce the risk of future misunderstandings. It also highlighted the crucial role of covert operatives in managing global crises, demonstrating that the shadowy world of espionage could be a force for peace as well as conflict.

The story of the Cuban Missile Crisis is a testament to the power of human ingenuity and courage in the face of unimaginable stakes. While the world remembers the public drama of the naval blockade and the televised speeches, it was the hidden efforts of the quiet men and women in the intelligence and diplomatic corps that secured the delicate peace. Their work reminds us that even in the darkest moments, the actions of a few can alter the course of history, saving countless lives and preserving the fragile balance of a world on the brink.

Epilogue: Guardians of the Shadows

Throughout the annals of history, the great tides of conflict and peace have often been shaped not by armies or treaties, but by those who operated in the shadows. Spies, covert operatives, and unsung negotiators have wielded their quiet influence to navigate the fault lines of power and avert catastrophes that would otherwise reshape the world. From ancient Rome to the Cold War, from the deserts of Persia to the storm-lashed beaches of Normandy, these figures have safeguarded nations and preserved lives, even as their names and deeds faded into the obscurity of classified archives.

Theirs is a world of paradox. The shadowy operatives who prevent wars often operate in the murky gray areas of morality, blurring the lines between right and wrong, truth and deception. They act not for glory or recognition, but for the stability and survival of a fragile order. Their triumphs are often invisible, their defeats catastrophic. Yet, their role is indispensable, for without them, the sharp edges of diplomacy would crumble, and the delicate balance of peace would falter.

History's great operatives have been many things: diplomats with silver tongues, spies with steel nerves, and strategists who saw beyond the horizon. They have worked in secret, weaving webs of alliances, feeding falsehoods to enemies, and collecting truths that empowered leaders to make decisions. They have toppled dictatorships, prevented invasions, and foiled plots that might have set the world ablaze. Yet, for all their influence, they remain ghosts in the grand narrative, their presence felt but rarely seen.

The enduring role of these guardians of the shadows is a testament to humanity's understanding that brute force alone cannot govern a complex world. Their stories remind us that wars are not inevitable, that conflicts can be shaped and resolved long before they explode into violence. Through their ingenuity and foresight, operatives have demonstrated time and again that peace, however fragile, can be maintained through the subtle art of espionage.

But the shadows they inhabit come with a cost. To serve as a guardian of peace often requires a willingness to sacrifice personal ideals, and sometimes personal lives, for the greater good. The operatives chronicled in these pages—whether they were sowing discord among enemy tribes, deceiving Nazi commanders, or maneuvering in the tense hours of the Cuban Missile Crisis—faced the unique burden of knowing their successes would remain unsung and their failures could shatter nations.

Even in the modern era, where technology has transformed the nature of intelligence work, the essence of their mission remains the same: to anticipate threats, manipulate outcomes, and protect the world from the brink. Satellites may replace pigeons, and code-breaking algorithms may outpace human cryptographers, but the role of the operative remains rooted in timeless skills—understanding people, navigating ambiguity, and playing the long game.

The lessons from their stories are as relevant today as they were in the past. They teach us that the best path to peace is not always the straightest one, that strategy often requires subtlety, and that understanding your adversary is as important as strength itself. Above all, they show that humanity's capacity for conflict is matched only by its capacity to seek resolution, even when the odds seem insurmountable.

As we step back and view the arc of history, it becomes clear that the guardians of the shadows are not relics of the past but enduring figures of the present and future. Their work continues, often unnoticed, in boardrooms, intelligence agencies, and back-channel negotiations. While the technologies and tactics may evolve, the essence of their mission remains timeless: to walk the shadowy path that holds the world together.

In the end, their legacy is not one of fame or glory, but of quiet impact. They remind us that peace is not a given—it is earned, protected, and preserved by those willing to work in the margins, unseen and uncelebrated. For every war that has been averted, for every conflict defused before it could ignite, we owe a debt to the invisible hands that steered history away from destruction.

To the operatives of the past and those still to come, the guardians of the shadows stand as a reminder of the quiet heroism required to secure the delicate peace upon which the world depends.